Edgar Allan Poe

Poet of the Macabre

Filiquarian Publishing, LLC.

Filiquarian Publishing, LLC is publishing this edition of Edgar Allan Poe – Poet of the Macabre, due to its status under the GNU Free Documentation License.

The cover of Edgar Allan Poe – Poet of the Macabre, and the "Biographiq" imprint is copyright 2008, Filiquarian Publishing, LLC.

Copyright (C) 2008 Filiquarian Publishing, LLC. Permission is granted to copy, distribute and/or modify this document under the terms of the GNU Free Documentation License, Version 1.2 or any later version published by the Free Software Foundation; with no Invariant Sections, no Front-Cover Texts, and no Back-Cover Texts. A copy of the license is included in the section entitled "GNU Free Documentation License".

Edgar Allan Poe – Poet of the Macabre
is available for free download at
www.biographiq.com/bookd/eappm216

Filiquarian Publishing, LLC.

Edgar Allan Poe
Poet of the Macabre

Edgar Allan Poe (January 19, 1809 – October 7, 1849) was an American poet, short-story writer, editor and literary critic, and is considered part of the American Romantic Movement. Best known for his tales of mystery and the macabre, Poe was one of the earliest American practitioners of the short story and invented the detective-fiction genre. He is credited with contributing to the emerging genre of science fiction.[1] He was the first well-known American writer to try to earn a living through writing alone, resulting in a financially difficult life and career.[2]

He was born Edgar Poe in Boston, Massachusetts. Poe, whose parents died when he was young, was taken in by John and Frances Allan, of Richmond,

Virginia but was never formally adopted by them. After spending a short period at the University of Virginia and briefly attempting a military career, Poe and the Allans parted ways. Poe's publishing career began humbly, with an anonymous collection of poems, Tamerlane and Other Poems (1827), credited only to "a Bostonian".

Poe switched his focus to prose and spent the next several years working for literary journals and periodicals, becoming known for his own style of literary criticism. His work forced him to move between several cities, including Baltimore, Philadelphia, Pennsylvania and New York City. In Baltimore in 1835, he married Virginia Clemm, his 13-year-old cousin. In January 1845, Poe published his poem "The Raven" to instant success. His wife died of tuberculosis two years later. He began planning to produce his own journal, The Penn (later renamed The Stylus), though he died before it could be produced. On October 7, 1849, at age 40, Poe died in Baltimore; the cause of his death is unknown and has been attributed to alcohol, brain congestion, cholera, drugs, heart disease, rabies, suicide, tuberculosis, and other agents.[3]

Poe and his works influenced literature in the United States and around the world, as well as in specialized fields, such as cosmology and cryptography. Poe and his work appear throughout popular culture in literature, music, films, and television. A number of his homes are dedicated museums today.

Life and Career

Early Life

Born Edgar Poe in Boston, Massachusetts, on January 19, 1809, the second child of actress Elizabeth Arnold Hopkins Poe and actor David Poe, Jr. He had an elder brother, William Henry Leonard Poe, and a younger sister, Rosalie Poe.[4] His father abandoned their family in 1810,[5] and his mother died a year later from consumption. Poe was then taken into the home of John Allan, a successful Scottish merchant in Richmond, Virginia, who dealt in a variety of goods including tobacco, cloth, wheat, tombstones, and slaves.[6] The Allans served as a foster family but never formally adopted Poe,[7] though they gave him the name "Edgar Allan Poe".[8]

The Allan family had Poe baptized in the Episcopal Church in 1812. John Allan alternately spoiled and aggressively disciplined his foster son.[8] The family, including Poe and Allan's wife, Frances Valentine Allan, sailed to England in 1815. Poe attended the grammar school in Irvine, Scotland (where John Allan was born) for a short period in 1815, before rejoining the family in London in 1816. He studied at a boarding school in Chelsea until summer 1817. He was subsequently entered at the Reverend John Bransby's Manor House School at Stoke Newington, then a suburb four miles (6 km) north of London.[9]

Poe moved back with the Allans to Richmond, Virginia in 1820. In 1825, John Allan's friend and business benefactor William Galt, said to be the wealthiest man in Richmond, died and left Allan several acres of real estate. The inheritance was estimated at $750,000. By summer 1825, Allan celebrated his expansive wealth by purchasing a two-story brick home named Moldavia.[10] Poe may have become engaged to Sarah Elmira Royster before he registered at the one-year old University of Virginia in February 1826 to study languages.[11] The university, in its infancy, was established on the ideals of its founder, Thomas Jefferson. It had strict rules against gambling, horses, guns, tobacco and alcohol, but these rules were generally ignored. Jefferson had enacted a system of student self-government, allowing students to choose their own studies, make their own arrangements for boarding, and report all wrongdoing to the faculty. The unique system was still in chaos, and there was a high drop-out rate.[12] During his time there, Poe lost touch with Royster and also became estranged from his foster father over gambling debts. Poe claimed that Allan had not given him sufficient money to register for classes, purchase texts, and procure and furnish a dormitory. Allan did send additional money and clothes, but Poe's debts increased.[13] Poe gave up on the university after a year, and, not feeling welcome in Richmond, especially when he learned that his sweetheart Royster had married Alexander Shelton, he traveled to Boston in April 1827, sustaining himself with odd jobs as a clerk and newspaper writer.[14] At some point he started using the pseudonym Henri Le Rennet.[15]

Military Career

Unable to support himself, on May 27, 1827, Poe enlisted in the United States Army as a private. Using the name "Edgar A. Perry", he claimed he was 22 years old even though he was 18.[16] He first served at Fort Independence in Boston Harbor for five dollars a month.[17] That same year, he released his first book, a 40-page collection of poetry, Tamerlane and Other Poems, attributed with the byline "by a Bostonian". Only 50 copies were printed, and the book received virtually no attention.[18] Poe's regiment was posted to Fort Moultrie in Charleston, South Carolina and traveled by ship on the brig Waltham on November 8, 1827. Poe was promoted to "artificer", an enlisted tradesman who prepared shells for artillery, and had his monthly pay doubled.[19] After serving for two years and attaining the rank of Sergeant Major for Artillery (the highest rank a noncommissioned officer can achieve), Poe sought to end his five-year enlistment early. He revealed his real name and his circumstances to his commanding officer, Lieutenant Howard, who would only allow Poe to be discharged if he reconciled with John Allan. Howard wrote a letter to Allan, who was unsympathetic. Several months passed and pleas to Allan were ignored; Allan may not have written to Poe even to make him aware of his foster mother's illness. Frances Allan died on February 28, 1829, and Poe visited the day after her burial. Perhaps softened by his wife's death, John Allan agreed to support Poe's attempt to be discharged in order to receive an appointment to the United States Military Academy at West Point.[20]

Poe finally was discharged on April 15, 1829, after securing a replacement to finish his enlisted term for him.[21] Before entering West Point, Poe moved back to Baltimore for a time, to stay with his widowed aunt Maria Clemm, her daughter, Virginia Eliza Clemm (Poe's first cousin), his brother Henry, and his invalid grandmother Elizabeth Cairnes Poe.[22] Meanwhile, Poe published his second book, Al Aaraaf, Tamerlane and Minor Poems, in Baltimore in 1829.[23]

Poe traveled to West Point and matriculated as a cadet on July 1, 1830.[24] In October 1830, John Allan married his second wife, Louisa Patterson.[25] The marriage, and bitter quarrels with Poe over the children born to Allan out of affairs, led to the foster father finally disowning Poe.[26] Poe decided to leave West Point by purposely getting court-martialed. On February 8, 1831, he was tried for gross neglect of duty and disobedience of orders for refusing to attend formations, classes, or church. Poe tactically pled not guilty to induce dismissal, knowing he would be found guilty.[27]

He left for New York in February 1831, and released a third volume of poems, simply titled Poems. The book was financed with help from his fellow cadets at West Point, many of whom donated 75 cents to the cause, raising a total of $170. They may have been expecting verses similar to the satirical ones Poe had been writing about commanding officers.[28] Printed by Elam Bliss of New York, it was labeled as "Second Edition" and included a page saying, "To the U.S. Corps of Cadets this volume is respectfully dedicated." The book once again reprinted the long poems "Tamerlane" and "Al Aaraaf" but also six previously unpublished poems including early versions of "To Helen", "Israfel", and "The City in the Sea".[29] He returned to Baltimore, to his aunt, brother and cousin, in March 1831. His elder brother Henry, who had been in ill health in part due to problems with alcoholism, died on August 1, 1831.[30]

Publishing Career

After his brother's death, Poe began more earnest attempts to start his career as a writer. He chose a difficult time in American publishing to do so.[31] He was the first well-known American to try to live by writing alone[2][32] and was hampered by the lack of an international copyright law.[33] Publishers often pirated copies of British works rather than paying for new work by Americans.[32] The industry was also particularly hurt by the Panic of 1837.[34] Despite a booming growth in American periodicals around this time period, fueled in part by new technology, many did not last beyond a few issues[35] and publishers often refused to pay their writers or paid them much later than they promised.[36] Poe, throughout his attempts at pursuing a successful literary career, would be forced to constantly make humiliating pleas for money and other assistance for the rest of his life.[37]

After his early attempts at poetry, Poe had turned his attention to prose. He placed a few stories with a Philadelphia publication and began work on his only drama, Politian. The Saturday Visitor, a Baltimore paper, awarded Poe a prize in October 1833 for his short story "MS. Found in a Bottle".[38] The story brought him to the attention of John P. Kennedy, a Baltimorian of considerable means. He helped Poe place some of his stories, and introduced him to Thomas W. White, editor of the Southern Literary Messenger in Richmond. Poe became assistant editor of the periodical in August 1835;[39] however, within a few weeks, he was discharged after being found drunk repeatedly.[40] Returning to Baltimore, Poe secretly married Virginia, his cousin, on September 22, 1835. She was 13 at the time, though she is listed on the marriage certificate as being 21.[41] Reinstated by White after promising good behavior, Poe went back to Richmond with Virginia and her mother. He remained at the

Messenger until January 1837. During this period, its circulation increased from 700 to 3,500.[4] He published several poems, book reviews, criticism, and stories in the paper. On May 16, 1836, he had a second wedding ceremony in Richmond with Virginia Clemm, this time in public.[42]

The Narrative of Arthur Gordon Pym was published and widely reviewed in 1838. In the summer of 1839, Poe became assistant editor of Burton's Gentleman's Magazine. He published a large number of articles, stories, and reviews, enhancing his reputation as a trenchant critic that he had established at the Southern Literary Messenger. Also in 1839, the collection Tales of the Grotesque and Arabesque was published in two volumes, though he made little money off of it and it received mixed reviews.[43] Poe left Burton's after about a year and found a position as assistant at Graham's Magazine.[44]

In June 1840, Poe published a prospectus announcing his intentions to start his own journal, The Stylus.[45] Originally, Poe intended to call the journal The Penn, as it would have been based in Philadelphia, Pennsylvania. In the June 6, 1840 issue of Philadelphia's Saturday Evening Post, Poe bought advertising space for his prospectus: "Prospectus of the Penn Magazine, a Monthly Literary journal to be edited and published in the city of Philadelphia by Edgar A. Poe."[46] The journal would never be produced before Poe's death. Around this time, he attempted to secure a position with the Tyler administration, claiming he was a member of the Whig Party.[47] He hoped to be appointed to the Custom House in Philadelphia with help from President Tyler's son Robert,[48] an acquaintance of Poe's friend Frederick Thomas.[49] Poe failed to show up for a meeting with Thomas to discuss the appointment in mid-September 1842, claiming to be sick, though Thomas believed he was drunk.[50] Though he was promised an appointment, all positions were filled by others.[51]

One evening in January 1842, Virginia showed the first signs of consumption, now known as tuberculosis, while singing and playing the piano. Poe described it as breaking a blood vessel in her throat.[52] She only partially recovered. Poe began to drink more heavily under the stress of Virginia's illness. He left Graham's and attempted to find a new position, for a time angling for a government post. He returned to New York, where he worked briefly at the Evening Mirror before becoming editor of the Broadway Journal and, later, sole owner.[53] There he alienated himself from other writers by publicly accusing Henry Wadsworth Longfellow of plagiarism, though Longfellow never responded.[54] On January 29, 1845, his poem "The Raven" appeared in the Evening Mirror and became a popular sensation. Though it made Poe a household name almost instantly,[55] he only was paid $9 for its publication.[56]

The Broadway Journal failed in 1846.[53] Poe moved to a cottage in the Fordham section of The Bronx, New York. That home, known today as the "Poe Cottage", is on the southeast corner of the Grand Concourse and Kingsbridge Road. Virginia died there on January 30, 1847.[57] Biographers and critics often suggest Poe's frequent theme of the "death of a beautiful woman" stems from the repeated loss of women throughout his life, including his wife.[58]

Increasingly unstable after his wife's death, Poe attempted to court the poet Sarah Helen Whitman, who lived in Providence, Rhode Island. Their engagement failed, purportedly because of Poe's drinking and erratic behavior. However, there is also strong evidence that Whitman's mother intervened and did much to derail their relationship.[59] Poe then returned to Richmond and resumed a relationship with a childhood sweetheart, Sarah Elmira Royster.[60]

Death

On October 3, 1849, Poe was found on the streets of Baltimore delirious, "in great distress, and... in need of immediate assistance", according to the man who found him, Joseph W. Walker.[61] He was taken to the Washington College Hospital, where he died on Sunday, October 7, 1849, at 5:00 in the morning.[62] Poe was never coherent long enough to explain how he came to be in his dire condition, and, oddly, was wearing clothes that were not his own. Poe is said to have repeatedly called out the name "Reynolds" on the night before his death, though it is unclear to whom he was referring. Some sources say Poe's final words were "Lord help my poor soul."[62] All medical records, including his death certificate, have been lost.[63] The precise cause of Poe's death remains a mystery.[64] Newspapers at the time reported Poe's death as "congestion of the brain" or "cerebral inflammation", common euphemisms for deaths from disgraceful causes such as alcoholism.[65] Many theories have been suggested, including delirium tremens, heart disease, epilepsy and meningeal inflammation.[66] One of the most common beliefs is that Poe was a victim of cooping, first suggested as early as 1872.[67]

Griswold's "Memoir"

The day Edgar Allan Poe was buried, a long obituary appeared in the New York Tribune signed "Ludwig". It was soon published throughout the country. The piece began, "Edgar Allan Poe is dead. He died in Baltimore the day before yesterday. This announcement will startle many, but few will be grieved by it."[68] "Ludwig" was soon identified as Rufus Wilmot Griswold, an editor, critic and anthologist who had borne a grudge against Poe since 1842. Griswold somehow became Poe's literary executor and attempted to destroy his enemy's reputation after his death.[69]

Rufus Griswold wrote a biographical article of Poe called "Memoir of the Author", which he included in an 1850 volume of the collected works. Griswold depicted Poe as a depraved, drunk, drug-addled madman and included Poe's letters as evidence.[69] Many of his claims were either outright lies or distorted half-truths. For example, it is now known that Poe was not a drug addict.[70] Griswold's book was denounced by those who knew Poe well,[71] but it became a popularly accepted one. This occurred in part because it was the only full biography available and was widely reprinted and in part because readers thrilled at the thought of reading works by an "evil" man.[72] Letters that Griswold presented as proof of this depiction of Poe were later revealed as forgeries.[73]

Edgar Allan Poe

Literary Style and Themes

Genres

Poe's best known fiction works are Gothic,[74] a genre he followed to appease the public taste.[75] His most recurring themes deal with questions of death, including its physical signs, the effects of decomposition, concerns of premature burial, the reanimation of the dead, and mourning.[76] Many of his works are generally considered part of the dark romanticism genre, a literary reaction to transcendentalism,[77] which Poe strongly disliked.[78] He referred to followers of the movement as "Frogpondians" after the pond on Boston Common.[79] and ridiculed their writings as "metaphor-run", lapsing into "obscurity for obscurity's sake" or "mysticism for mysticism's sake."[80] Poe once wrote in a letter to Thomas Holley Chivers that he did not dislike Transcendentalists, "only the pretenders and sophists among them."[81]

Beyond horror, Poe also wrote satires, humor tales, and hoaxes. For comic effect, he used irony and ludicrous extravagance, often in an attempt to liberate the reader from cultural conformity.[75] In fact, "Metzengerstein", the first story that Poe is known to have published,[82] and his first foray into horror, was originally intended as a burlesque satirizing the popular genre.[83] Poe also reinvented science fiction, responding in his writing to emerging technologies such as hot air balloons in "The Balloon-Hoax".[84]

Poe wrote much of his work using themes specifically catered for mass market tastes.[85] To that end, his fiction often included elements of popular pseudosciences such as phrenology[86] and physiognomy.[87]

Literary Theory

Poe's writing reflects his literary theories, which he presented in his criticism and also in essays such as "The Poetic Principle".[88] He disliked didacticism[89] and allegory,[90] though he believed that meaning in literature should be an undercurrent just beneath the surface. Works with obvious meanings, he wrote, cease to be art.[91] He believed that quality work should be brief and focus on a specific single effect.[92] To that end, he believed that the writer should carefully calculate every sentiment and idea.[93] In "The Philosophy of Composition", an essay in which Poe describes his method in writing "The Raven", he claims to have strictly followed this method. It has been questioned, however, if he really followed this system. T. S. Eliot said: "It is difficult for us to read that essay without reflecting that if Poe plotted out his poem with such calculation, he might have taken a little more pains over it: the result hardly does credit to the method."[94] Biographer Joseph Wood Krutch described the essay as "a rather highly ingenious exercise in the art of rationalization".[95]

Legacy

Literary Influence

During his lifetime, Poe was mostly recognized as a literary critic. Fellow critic James Russell Lowell called him "the most discriminating, philosophical, and fearless critic upon imaginative works who has written in America", though he questioned if he occasionally used prussic acid instead of ink.[96] Poe was also known as a writer of fiction and became one of the first American authors of the 19th century to become more popular in Europe than in the United States.[97] Poe is particularly respected in France, in part due to early translations by Charles Baudelaire. Baudelaire's translations quickly became definitive renditions of Poe's work throughout Europe.[98]

Poe's early detective fiction tales starring the fictitious C. Auguste Dupin laid the groundwork for future detectives in literature. Sir Arthur Conan Doyle said, "Each [of Poe's detective stories] is a root from which a whole literature has developed.... Where was the detective story until Poe breathed the breath of life into it?"[99] The Mystery Writers of America have named their awards for excellence in the genre the "Edgars".[100] Poe's work also influenced science fiction, notably Jules Verne, who wrote a sequel to Poe's novel The Narrative of Arthur Gordon Pym of Nantucket called The Narrative of Arthur Gordon Pym, Le sphinx des glaces.[101] Science fiction author H. G. Wells noted, "Pym tells what a very intelligent mind could imagine about the south polar region a century ago."[102]

Like many famous artists, Poe's works have spawned innumerable imitators.[103] One interesting trend among imitators of Poe, however, has been claims by clairvoyants or psychics to be "channeling" poems from Poe's spirit beyond the grave. One of the most notable of these was Lizzie Doten, who in 1863 published Poems from the Inner Life, in which she claimed to have "received" new compositions by Poe's spirit. The compositions were re-workings of famous Poe poems such as "The Bells", but which reflected a new, positive outlook.[104]

Even so, Poe has not received only praise. William Butler Yeats was generally critical of Poe, calling him "vulgar".[105] Transcendentalist Ralph Waldo Emerson reacted to "The Raven" by saying, "I see nothing in it"[106] and derisively referred to Poe as "the jingle man".[107] Aldous Huxley wrote that Poe's writing "falls into vulgarity" by being "too poetical" - the equivalent of wearing a diamond ring on every finger.[108]

Physics and Cosmology

Eureka: A Prose Poem, an essay written in 1848, included a cosmological theory that presaged the big bang theory by 80 years,[109] as well as the first plausible solution to Olbers' paradox.[110] Poe eschewed the scientific method in Eureka and instead wrote from pure intuition.[111] For this reason, he considered it a work of art, not science,[111] but insisted that it was still true[112] and considered it to be his career masterpiece.[113] Even so, Eureka is full of scientific errors. In particular, Poe's suggestions opposed Newtonian principles regarding the density and rotation of planets.[114]

Cryptography

Poe had a keen interest in the field of cryptography. He had placed a notice of his abilities in the Philadelphia paper Alexander's Weekly (Express) Messenger, inviting submissions of ciphers, which he proceeded to solve.[115] In July 1841, Poe had published an essay called "A Few Words on Secret Writing" in Graham's Magazine. Realizing the public interest in the topic, he wrote "The Gold-Bug" incorporating ciphers as part of the story.[116] Poe's success in cryptography relied not so much on his knowledge of that field (his method was limited to the simple substitution cryptogram), as on his knowledge of the magazine and newspaper culture. His keen analytical abilities, which were so evident in his detective stories, allowed him to see that the general public was largely ignorant of the methods by which a simple substitution cryptogram can be solved, and he used this to his advantage.[115] The sensation Poe created with his cryptography stunt played a major role in popularizing cryptograms in newspapers and magazines.[117]

Poe had an influence on cryptography beyond increasing public interest in his lifetime. William Friedman, America's foremost cryptologist, was heavily influenced by Poe.[118] Friedman's initial interest in cryptography came from reading "The Gold-Bug" as a child — interest he later put to use in deciphering Japan's PURPLE code during World War II.[119]

Poe in Popular Culture

Poe as a Character

The historical Edgar Allan Poe has appeared as a fictionalized character, often representing the "mad genius" or "tormented artist" and exploiting his personal struggles.[120] Many such depictions also blend in with characters from his stories, suggesting Poe and his characters share identities.[121] Often, fictional depictions of Poe use his mystery-solving skills in such novels as The Poe Shadow by Matthew Pearl.[122]

Preserved Homes, Landmarks, and Museums

No childhood home of Poe is still standing, including the Allan family's Moldavia estate. The oldest standing home in Richmond, the Old Stone House, is in use as the Edgar Allan Poe Museum, though Poe never lived there. The collection includes many items Poe used during his time with the Allan family and also features several rare first printings of Poe works. The dorm room Poe is believed to have used while studying at the University of Virginia in 1826 is preserved and available for visits. Its upkeep is now overseen by a group of students and staff known as the Raven Society.[123]

The earliest surviving home in which Poe lived is in Baltimore, preserved as the Edgar Allan Poe House and Museum. Poe is believed to have lived in the home at the age of 23 when he first lived with Maria Clemm and Virginia (as well as his grandmother and possibly his brother William Henry Leonard Poe). It is open to the public and is also the home of the Edgar Allan Poe Society. Of the several homes that Poe, his wife Virginia, and his mother-in-law Maria rented in Philadelphia, only the last house has survived. The Spring Garden home, where the author lived in 1843 – 44, is today preserved by the National Park Service as the Edgar Allan Poe National Historic Site. Poe's final home is preserved as the Poe Cottage in the Bronx, New York.[57][124]

Other Poe landmarks include a building in the Upper West Side, where Poe temporarily lived when he first moved to New York. A plaque suggests that Poe wrote "The Raven" here. In Boston, a plaque hangs near the building where

Poe was born once stood. Believed to have been located at 62 Carver Street (now Charles Street), the plaque is possibly in an incorrect location.[125][126] The bar in which legend says Poe was last seen drinking before his death still stands in Fells Point in Baltimore, Maryland. Now known as The Horse You Came In On, local lore insists that a ghost they call "Edgar" haunts the rooms above.[127]

Poe Toaster

Adding to the mystery surrounding Poe's death, an unknown visitor affectionately referred to as the "Poe Toaster" has paid homage to Poe's grave every year since 1949. As the tradition has been carried on for more than 50 years, it is likely that the "Poe Toaster" is actually several individuals; however, the tribute is always the same. Every January 19, in the early hours of the morning, the man makes a toast of cognac to Poe's original grave marker and leaves three roses. Members of the Edgar Allan Poe Society in Baltimore have helped in protecting this tradition for decades. On August 15, 2007, Sam Porpora, a former historian at the Westminster Church in Baltimore where

Poe is buried, claimed that he had started the tradition in the 1960s. The claim that the tradition began in 1949, he said, was a hoax in order to raise money and enhance the profile of the church. His story has not been confirmed,[128] and some details he has given to the press have been pointed out as factually inaccurate.[129]

Selected List of Works

Tales

* "Berenice"

* "The Black Cat"

* "The Cask of Amontillado"

* "The Fall of the House of Usher"

* "The Gold-Bug"

* "Hop-Frog"

* "Ligeia"

* "The Man of the Crowd"

* "The Masque of the Red Death"

* "The Murders in the Rue Morgue"

* "The Pit and the Pendulum"

* "The Purloined Letter"

* "The Tell-Tale Heart"

* "The Oblong Box"

* "The Premature Burial"

* "The Oval Portrait"

Poetry

* "A Dream Within A Dream"

* "Annabel Lee"

* "The Bells"

* "The City in the Sea"

* "The Conqueror Worm"

* "Eldorado"

* "The Haunted Palace"

* "Lenore"

* "The Raven"

* "Ulalume"

Other Works

* The Narrative of Arthur Gordon Pym of Nantucket (1838) – Poe's only complete novel

* "The Balloon-Hoax" (1844) – A journalistic hoax printed as a true story

* "The Philosophy of Composition" (1846) – Essay

* Eureka: A Prose Poem (1848) – Essay

Poet of the Macabre

References

Notes

1. Stableford, Brian. "Science fiction before the genre." The Cambridge Companion to Science Fiction, Eds. Edward James and Farah Mendlesohn. Cambridge: Cambridge University of Press, 2003. pp. 18 – 19.

2. Meyers, 138

3. Meyers, 256

4. Allen, Hervey. "Introduction". The Works of Edgar Allan Poe, New York: P. F. Collier & Son, 1927.

5. Canada, Mark, ed. "Edgar Allan Poe Chronology". Canada's America. 1997. Retrieved on 3 June 2007.

6. Meyers, 8

7. Quinn, 61

8. Meyers, 9

9. Silverman, 16 – 18

10. Silverman, 27 – 28

11. Silverman, 29 – 30

12. Meyers, 21 – 22

13. Silverman, 32 – 34

14. Meyers, 32

15. Silverman, 41

16. Cornelius, Kay. "Biography of Edgar Allan Poe", Bloom's BioCritiques: Edgar Allan Poe, Ed. Harold Bloom, Philadelphia: Chelsea House Publishers, 2002. p. 13 ISBN 0791061736

17. Meyers, 32

18. Meyers, 33 – 34

19. Meyers, 35

20. Silverman, 43 – 47

21. Meyers, 38

22. Cornelius, Kay. "Biography of Edgar Allan Poe", Bloom's BioCritiques: Edgar Allan Poe, Ed. Harold Bloom, Philadelphia: Chelsea House Publishers, 2002. pp. 13 – 14 ISBN 0791061736

23. Sova, 5

24. Krutch, 32

25. Cornelius, Kay. "Biography of Edgar Allan Poe", Bloom's BioCritiques: Edgar Allan Poe, Ed. Harold Bloom, Philadelphia: Chelsea House Publishers, 2002. p. 14 ISBN 0791061736

26. Meyers, 54 – 55

27. Hecker, William J. Private Perry and Mister Poe: The West Point Poems. Louisiana State University Press, 2005. pp. 49 – 51

28. Meyers, 50 – 51

29. Hecker, William J. Private Perry and Mister Poe: The West Point Poems. Louisiana State University Press, 2005. pp. 53 – 54

30. Quinn, 187 – 188

31. Whalen, 64

32. Quinn, 305

33. Silverman, 247

34. Whalen, 74

35. Silverman, 99

36. Whalen, 82

37. Meyers, 139

38. Sova, 162

39. Sova, 225

40. Meyers, 73

41. Meyers, 85

42. Silverman, 124

43. Meyers, 113

44. Sova, 39, 99

45. Meyers, 119

46. Silverman, 159

47. Quinn, 321 – 322

48. Silverman, 186

49. Meyers, 144

50. Silverman, 187

51. Silverman, 188

52. Silverman, 179

53. Sova, 34

54. Quinn, 455

55. Hoffman, 80

56. Ostrom, John Ward. "Edgar A. Poe: His Income as Literary Entrepreneur", Poe Studies 5.1 (1982): 5

57. Edgar Allan Poe Cottage. Bronx Historical Society. Retrieved on 2007-10-13.

58. Weekes, Karen. "Poe's feminine ideal," The Cambridge Companion to Edgar Allan Poe, Ed. Kevin J. Hayes. Cambridge University Press, 2002. p. 149. ISBN 0521797276

59. Benton, Richard P. "Friends and Enemies: Women in the Life of Edgar Allan Poe", Myths and Reality: The Mysterious Mr. Poe. Baltimore: Edgar Allan Poe Society, 1987. p. 19 ISBN 0961644915

60. Quinn, 628

61. Quinn, 638

62. Meyers, 255

63. Bramsback, Birgit (1970). "The Final Illness and Death of Edgar Allan Poe: An Attempt at Reassessment", Studia Neophilologica (University of Uppsala), XLII. p. 40

64. Silverman, 435

65. Silverman, 435 – 436

66. Meyers, 256

67. Walsh, John Evangelist (2000). Midnight Dreary: The Mysterious Death of Edgar Allan Poe, Paperback ed., New York: St. Martin's Minotaur, 32 –33. ISBN 0312227329.

68. Meyers, 259. To read Griswold's full obituary, see Edgar Allan Poe obituary at Wikisource.

69. Hoffman, 14

70. Quinn, 693

71. Sova, 101

72. Meyers, 263

73. Quinn, 699

74. Meyers, 64

75. Royot, Daniel (2002). "Poe's Humor", The Cambridge Companion to Edgar Allan Poe. Cambridge University Press. ISBN 0521797276. p. 57.

76. Kennedy, J. Gerald (1987). Poe, Death, and the Life of Writing. Yale University Press. ISBN 0300037732. p. 3.

77. Koster, Donald N. (2002). "Influences of Transcendentalism on American Life and Literature", Literary Movements for Students Vol.1. David Galens, ed. Detroit: Thompson Gale. p. 336.

78. Ljunquist, Kent (2002). "The poet as critic", The Cambridge Companion to Edgar Allan Poe,

Kevin J. Hayes, ed. Cambridge University Press.
ISBN 0521797276 p. 15

79. Royot, Daniel. "Poe's humor," as collected in
The Cambridge Companion to Edgar Allan Poe,
Kevin J. Hayes, ed. Cambridge University Press,
2002. pp. 61 –62. ISBN 0521797276

80. Ljunquist, Kent. "The poet as critic" collected
in The Cambridge Companion to Edgar Allan Poe,
Kevin J. Hayes, ed. Cambridge University Press,
2002. p.15. ISBN 0521797276

81. Silverman, 169

82. Silverman, 88

83. Fisher, Benjamin Franklin (1993). "Poe's
'Metzengerstein': Not a Hoax", On Poe: The Best
from "American Literature. Durham, NC: Duke
University Press. p. 142, 149

84. Tresch, John (2002). "Extra! Extra! Poe
invents science fiction!", The Cambridge
Companion to Edgar Allan Poe, Kevin J. Hayes,

ed. Cambridge University Press. ISBN 0521797276. p. 114.

85. Whalen, 67

86. Edward Hungerford (1930). "Poe and Phrenology", American Literature Vol.1. p. 209 – 31.

87. Erik Grayson (2005). "Weird Science, Weirder Unity: Phrenology and Physiognomy in Edgar Allan Poe", Mode Vol. 1 p. 56 – 77.

88. Krutch, 225

89. Kagle, Steven E. "The Corpse Within Us", Poe and His Times: The Artist and His Milieu, Ed. Benjamin Franklin Fisher IV. Baltimore: The Edgar Allan Poe Society, Inc., 1990. ISBN 0961644923. p. 104

90. Poe, Edgar A.. Tale-Writing — Nathaniel Hawthorne. Godey's Lady's Book, November 1847, pp. 252 – 256. Retrieved on 2007-03-24.

91. Wilbur, Richard (1967). "The House of Poe", Poe: A Collection of Critical Essays, Ed. Robert Regan. Englewood Cliffs, NJ: Prentice-Hall, Inc. p. 99

92. Krutch, 225

93. Jannaccone, Pasquale (translated by Peter Mitilineos) (1974). "The Aesthetics of Edgar Poe", Poe Studies Vol. 7.1. p. 3.

94. Hoffman, 76

95. Krutch, 98

96. Quinn, 432

97. Meyers, 258

98. Harner, Gary Wayne. "Edgar Allan Poe in France: Baudelaire's Labor of Love", Poe and His Times: The Artist and His Milieu, Ed. Benjamin Franklin Fisher IV. Baltimore: The Edgar Allan Poe Society, 1990. p. 218. ISBN 0961644923

99. Poe Encyclopedia, 103

100. Neimeyer, Mark. "Poe and Popular Culture," Ed. Kevin J. Hayes. The Cambridge Companion to Edgar Allan Poe. Cambridge University Press, 2002. ISBN 0521797276 p. 206

101. Poe Encyclopedia, 364

102. Poe Encyclopedia, 372

103. Meyers, 281

104. Carlson, Eric Walter (1996). A Companion to Poe Studies. Westport, Connecticut: Greenwood Press, 476. ISBN 0-313-26506-2.

105. Meyers, 274

106. Silverman, 265

107. Emerson's Estimate of Poe. Retrieved on 2008-03-02.

108. Huxley, Aldous. "Vulgarity in Literature," Poe: A Collection of Critical Essays, Ed. Robert

Regan, Englewood Cliffs, NJ: Prentice-Hall Inc., 1967. p. 32

109. Rombeck, Terry. "Poe's little-known science book reprinted", Lawrence Journal-World & News. January 22, 2005

110. Smoot, George and Keay Davidson. Wrinkles in Time. Harper Perennial, Reprint edition (October 1, 1994) ISBN 0-380-72044-2
111.Meyers, 214

112. Silverman, 399

113. Meyers, 219

114. Sova, 82 115.Silverman, 152

116. Rosenheim, 2, 6

117. Friedman, William F. "Edgar Allan Poe, Cryptographer", On Poe: The Best from "American Literature". Durham, NC: Duke University Press, 1993. p. 40 – 41

118. Rosenheim, 15

119. Rosenheim, 146

120. Neimeyer, Mark. "Poe and Popular Culture", The Cambridge Companion to Edgar Allan Poe. Cambridge University Press, 2002. ISBN 0521797276 p. 209

121. Gargano, James W. "The Question of Poe's Narrators," Poe: A Collection of Critical Essays, Ed. Robert Regan. Englewood Cliffs, NJ: Prentice-Hall, Inc., 1967. p. 165

122. Maslin, Janet. "The Poe Shadow", International Herald Tribune, 2006-06-06. Retrieved on 2007-10-13.

123. Raven Society Homepage. University of Virginia. Retrieved on 16 December 2007.

124. Burns, Niccole. "Poe wrote most important works in Philadelphia", School of Communication - University of Miami, 2006-11-15. Retrieved on 2007-10-13.

125. Van Hoy, David C. "The Fall of the House of Edgar". The Boston Globe, February 18, 2007

126. Glenn, Joshua. The house of Poe -- mystery solved! The Boston Globe April 9, 2007

127. Lake, Matt. Weird Maryland. Sterling Publishing, New York, 2006. ISBN 1402739060 p. 195.

128. Hall, Wiley. "Poe Fan Takes Credit for Grave Legend," Associated Press, August 15, 2007.

129. Associated Press (August 15, 2007). Man Reveals Legend of Mystery Visitor to Edgar Allan Poe's Grave. FoxNews.com. Retrieved on 2007-12-15.

Poet of the Macabre

General References

* Foye, Raymond (editor) (1980). The Unknown Poe, Paperback ed., San Francisco, CA: City Lights. ISBN 0872861104.

* Frank, Fredierck S.; Anthony Magistrale (1997). The Poe Encyclopedia. Westport, CT: Greenwood Press. ISBN 0313277680.

* Hoffman, Daniel (1998). Poe Poe Poe Poe Poe Poe Poe, Paperback ed., Baton Rouge, La.: Louisiana State University Press. ISBN 0807123218.

* Krutch, Joseph Wood (1926). Edgar Allan Poe: A Study in Genius. New York: Alfred A. Knopf.

* Meyers, Jeffrey (1992). Edgar Allan Poe: His Life and Legacy, Paperback ed., New York: Cooper Square Press. ISBN 0815410387.

* Quinn, Arthur Hobson (1941). Edgar Allan Poe: A Critical Biography. New York: Appleton-Century-Crofts, Inc.. ISBN 0801857309.

* Rosenheim, Shawn James (1997). The Cryptographic Imagination: Secret Writing from Edgar Poe to the Internet. Baltimore: Johns Hopkins University Press. ISBN 9780801853326.

* Silverman, Kenneth (1991). Edgar A. Poe: Mournful and Never-Ending Remembrance, Paperback ed., New York: Harper Perennial. ISBN 0060923318.

* Sova, Dawn B. (2001). Edgar Allan Poe: A to Z, Paperback ed., New York: Checkmark Books. ISBN 081604161X.

* Whalen, Terence (2001). "Poe and the American Publishing Industry", A Historical Guide to Edgar Allan Poe. New York: Oxford University Press. ISBN 0195121503

Edgar Allan Poe

GNU Free Documentation License

Version 1.2, November 2002

Copyright (C) 2000,2001,2002 Free Software Foundation, Inc.
51 Franklin St, Fifth Floor, Boston, MA 02110-1301 USA
Everyone is permitted to copy and distribute verbatim copies of this license document, but changing it is not allowed.

0. PREAMBLE

The purpose of this License is to make a manual, textbook, or other functional and useful document "free" in the sense of freedom: to assure everyone the effective freedom to copy and redistribute it, with or without modifying it, either commercially or noncommercially. Secondarily, this License preserves for the author and publisher a way to get credit for their work, while not being considered responsible for modifications made by others.

This License is a kind of "copyleft", which means that derivative works of the document must themselves be free in the same sense. It complements the GNU General Public License, which is a copyleft license designed for free software.

We have designed this License in order to use it for manuals for free software, because free software needs free documentation: a free program should come with manuals providing the same freedoms that the software does. But this License is not limited to software manuals; it can be used for any textual work, regardless of subject matter or whether it is published as a printed book. We recommend this License principally for works whose purpose is instruction or reference.

Poet of the Macabre

1. APPLICABILITY AND DEFINITIONS

This License applies to any manual or other work, in any medium, that contains a notice placed by the copyright holder saying it can be distributed under the terms of this License. Such a notice grants a world-wide, royalty-free license, unlimited in duration, to use that work under the conditions stated herein. The "Document", below, refers to any such manual or work. Any member of the public is a licensee, and is addressed as "you". You accept the license if you copy, modify or distribute the work in a way requiring permission under copyright law.

A "Modified Version" of the Document means any work containing the Document or a portion of it, either copied verbatim, or with modifications and/or translated into another language.

A "Secondary Section" is a named appendix or a front-matter section of the Document that deals exclusively with the relationship of the publishers or authors of the Document to the Document's overall subject (or to related matters) and contains nothing that could fall directly within that overall subject. (Thus, if the Document is in part a textbook of mathematics, a Secondary Section may not explain any mathematics.) The relationship could be a matter of historical connection with the subject or with related matters, or of legal, commercial, philosophical, ethical or political position regarding them.

The "Invariant Sections" are certain Secondary Sections whose titles are designated, as being those of Invariant Sections, in the notice that says that the Document is released under this License. If a section does not fit the above definition of Secondary then it is not allowed to be designated as Invariant. The Document may contain zero Invariant Sections. If the Document does not identify any Invariant Sections then there are none.

The "Cover Texts" are certain short passages of text that are listed, as Front-Cover Texts or Back-Cover Texts, in the notice that says that the Document is released under this License. A Front-Cover Text may be at most 5 words, and a Back-Cover Text may be at most 25 words.

Edgar Allan Poe

A "Transparent" copy of the Document means a machine-readable copy, represented in a format whose specification is available to the general public, that is suitable for revising the document straightforwardly with generic text editors or (for images composed of pixels) generic paint programs or (for drawings) some widely available drawing editor, and that is suitable for input to text formatters or for automatic translation to a variety of formats suitable for input to text formatters. A copy made in an otherwise Transparent file format whose markup, or absence of markup, has been arranged to thwart or discourage subsequent modification by readers is not Transparent. An image format is not Transparent if used for any substantial amount of text. A copy that is not "Transparent" is called "Opaque".

Examples of suitable formats for Transparent copies include plain ASCII without markup, Texinfo input format, LaTeX input format, SGML or XML using a publicly available DTD, and standard-conforming simple HTML, PostScript or PDF designed for human modification. Examples of transparent image formats include PNG, XCF and JPG. Opaque formats include proprietary formats that can be read and edited only by proprietary word processors, SGML or XML for which the DTD and/or processing tools are not generally available, and the machine-generated HTML, PostScript or PDF produced by some word processors for output purposes only.

The "Title Page" means, for a printed book, the title page itself, plus such following pages as are needed to hold, legibly, the material this License requires to appear in the title page. For works in formats which do not have any title page as such, "Title Page" means the text near the most prominent appearance of the work's title, preceding the beginning of the body of the text.

A section "Entitled XYZ" means a named subunit of the Document whose title either is precisely XYZ or contains XYZ in parentheses following text that translates XYZ in another language. (Here XYZ stands for a specific section name mentioned below, such as "Acknowledgements", "Dedications", "Endorsements", or "History".) To "Preserve the Title" of such a section when you modify the Document means that it remains a section "Entitled XYZ" according to this definition.

Poet of the Macabre

The Document may include Warranty Disclaimers next to the notice which states that this License applies to the Document. These Warranty Disclaimers are considered to be included by reference in this License, but only as regards disclaiming warranties: any other implication that these Warranty Disclaimers may have is void and has no effect on the meaning of this License.

2. VERBATIM COPYING

You may copy and distribute the Document in any medium, either commercially or noncommercially, provided that this License, the copyright notices, and the license notice saying this License applies to the Document are reproduced in all copies, and that you add no other conditions whatsoever to those of this License. You may not use technical measures to obstruct or control the reading or further copying of the copies you make or distribute. However, you may accept compensation in exchange for copies. If you distribute a large enough number of copies you must also follow the conditions in section 3.

You may also lend copies, under the same conditions stated above, and you may publicly display copies.

3. COPYING IN QUANTITY

If you publish printed copies (or copies in media that commonly have printed covers) of the Document, numbering more than 100, and the Document's license notice requires Cover Texts, you must enclose the copies in covers that carry, clearly and legibly, all these Cover Texts: Front-Cover Texts on the front cover, and Back-Cover Texts on the back cover. Both covers must also clearly and legibly identify you as the publisher of these copies. The front cover must present the full title with all words of the title equally prominent and visible. You may add other material on the covers in addition. Copying with changes limited to the covers, as long as they preserve the title of the Document and satisfy these conditions, can be treated as verbatim copying in other respects.

If the required texts for either cover are too voluminous to fit legibly, you should put the first ones listed (as many as fit reasonably) on the actual cover, and continue the rest onto adjacent pages.

Edgar Allan Poe

If you publish or distribute Opaque copies of the Document numbering more than 100, you must either include a machine-readable Transparent copy along with each Opaque copy, or state in or with each Opaque copy a computer-network location from which the general network-using public has access to download using public-standard network protocols a complete Transparent copy of the Document, free of added material. If you use the latter option, you must take reasonably prudent steps, when you begin distribution of Opaque copies in quantity, to ensure that this Transparent copy will remain thus accessible at the stated location until at least one year after the last time you distribute an Opaque copy (directly or through your agents or retailers) of that edition to the public.

It is requested, but not required, that you contact the authors of the Document well before redistributing any large number of copies, to give them a chance to provide you with an updated version of the Document.

4. MODIFICATIONS

You may copy and distribute a Modified Version of the Document under the conditions of sections 2 and 3 above, provided that you release the Modified Version under precisely this License, with the Modified Version filling the role of the Document, thus licensing distribution and modification of the Modified Version to whoever possesses a copy of it. In addition, you must do these things in the Modified Version:

* A. Use in the Title Page (and on the covers, if any) a title distinct from that of the Document, and from those of previous versions (which should, if there were any, be listed in the History section of the Document). You may use the same title as a previous version if the original publisher of that version gives permission.
* B. List on the Title Page, as authors, one or more persons or entities responsible for authorship of the modifications in the Modified Version, together with at least five of the principal authors of the Document (all of its principal authors, if it has fewer than five), unless they release you from this requirement.
* C. State on the Title page the name of the publisher of the Modified Version, as the publisher.
* D. Preserve all the copyright notices of the Document.

Poet of the Macabre

* E. Add an appropriate copyright notice for your modifications adjacent to the other copyright notices.
* F. Include, immediately after the copyright notices, a license notice giving the public permission to use the Modified Version under the terms of this License, in the form shown in the Addendum below.
* G. Preserve in that license notice the full lists of Invariant Sections and required Cover Texts given in the Document's license notice.
* H. Include an unaltered copy of this License.
* I. Preserve the section Entitled "History", Preserve its Title, and add to it an item stating at least the title, year, new authors, and publisher of the Modified Version as given on the Title Page. If there is no section Entitled "History" in the Document, create one stating the title, year, authors, and publisher of the Document as given on its Title Page, then add an item describing the Modified Version as stated in the previous sentence.
* J. Preserve the network location, if any, given in the Document for public access to a Transparent copy of the Document, and likewise the network locations given in the Document for previous versions it was based on. These may be placed in the "History" section. You may omit a network location for a work that was published at least four years before the Document itself, or if the original publisher of the version it refers to gives permission.
* K. For any section Entitled "Acknowledgements" or "Dedications", Preserve the Title of the section, and preserve in the section all the substance and tone of each of the contributor acknowledgements and/or dedications given therein.
* L. Preserve all the Invariant Sections of the Document, unaltered in their text and in their titles. Section numbers or the equivalent are not considered part of the section titles.
* M. Delete any section Entitled "Endorsements". Such a section may not be included in the Modified Version.
* N. Do not retitle any existing section to be Entitled "Endorsements" or to conflict in title with any Invariant Section.
* O. Preserve any Warranty Disclaimers.

If the Modified Version includes new front-matter sections or appendices that qualify as Secondary Sections and contain no material copied from the Document, you may at your option designate some or all of these sections as invariant. To do this, add their titles to the list of Invariant Sections in the

Edgar Allan Poe

Modified Version's license notice. These titles must be distinct from any other section titles.

You may add a section Entitled "Endorsements", provided it contains nothing but endorsements of your Modified Version by various parties--for example, statements of peer review or that the text has been approved by an organization as the authoritative definition of a standard.

You may add a passage of up to five words as a Front-Cover Text, and a passage of up to 25 words as a Back-Cover Text, to the end of the list of Cover Texts in the Modified Version. Only one passage of Front-Cover Text and one of Back-Cover Text may be added by (or through arrangements made by) any one entity. If the Document already includes a cover text for the same cover, previously added by you or by arrangement made by the same entity you are acting on behalf of, you may not add another; but you may replace the old one, on explicit permission from the previous publisher that added the old one.

The author(s) and publisher(s) of the Document do not by this License give permission to use their names for publicity for or to assert or imply endorsement of any Modified Version.

5. COMBINING DOCUMENTS

You may combine the Document with other documents released under this License, under the terms defined in section 4 above for modified versions, provided that you include in the combination all of the Invariant Sections of all of the original documents, unmodified, and list them all as Invariant Sections of your combined work in its license notice, and that you preserve all their Warranty Disclaimers.

The combined work need only contain one copy of this License, and multiple identical Invariant Sections may be replaced with a single copy. If there are multiple Invariant Sections with the same name but different contents, make the title of each such section unique by adding at the end of it, in parentheses, the name of the original author or publisher of that section if known, or else a unique number. Make the same adjustment to the section titles in the list of Invariant Sections in the license notice of the combined work.

Poet of the Macabre

In the combination, you must combine any sections Entitled "History" in the various original documents, forming one section Entitled "History"; likewise combine any sections Entitled "Acknowledgements", and any sections Entitled "Dedications". You must delete all sections Entitled "Endorsements."

6. COLLECTIONS OF DOCUMENTS

You may make a collection consisting of the Document and other documents released under this License, and replace the individual copies of this License in the various documents with a single copy that is included in the collection, provided that you follow the rules of this License for verbatim copying of each of the documents in all other respects.

You may extract a single document from such a collection, and distribute it individually under this License, provided you insert a copy of this License into the extracted document, and follow this License in all other respects regarding verbatim copying of that document.

7. AGGREGATION WITH INDEPENDENT WORKS

A compilation of the Document or its derivatives with other separate and independent documents or works, in or on a volume of a storage or distribution medium, is called an "aggregate" if the copyright resulting from the compilation is not used to limit the legal rights of the compilation's users beyond what the individual works permit. When the Document is included in an aggregate, this License does not apply to the other works in the aggregate which are not themselves derivative works of the Document.

If the Cover Text requirement of section 3 is applicable to these copies of the Document, then if the Document is less than one half of the entire aggregate, the Document's Cover Texts may be placed on covers that bracket the Document within the aggregate, or the electronic equivalent of covers if the Document is in electronic form. Otherwise they must appear on printed covers that bracket the whole aggregate.

Edgar Allan Poe

8. TRANSLATION

Translation is considered a kind of modification, so you may distribute translations of the Document under the terms of section 4. Replacing Invariant Sections with translations requires special permission from their copyright holders, but you may include translations of some or all Invariant Sections in addition to the original versions of these Invariant Sections. You may include a translation of this License, and all the license notices in the Document, and any Warranty Disclaimers, provided that you also include the original English version of this License and the original versions of those notices and disclaimers. In case of a disagreement between the translation and the original version of this License or a notice or disclaimer, the original version will prevail.

If a section in the Document is Entitled "Acknowledgements", "Dedications", or "History", the requirement (section 4) to Preserve its Title (section 1) will typically require changing the actual title.

9. TERMINATION

You may not copy, modify, sublicense, or distribute the Document except as expressly provided for under this License. Any other attempt to copy, modify, sublicense or distribute the Document is void, and will automatically terminate your rights under this License. However, parties who have received copies, or rights, from you under this License will not have their licenses terminated so long as such parties remain in full compliance.

10. FUTURE REVISIONS OF THIS LICENSE

The Free Software Foundation may publish new, revised versions of the GNU Free Documentation License from time to time. Such new versions will be similar in spirit to the present version, but may differ in detail to address new problems or concerns. See http://www.gnu.org/copyleft/.

Each version of the License is given a distinguishing version number. If the Document specifies that a particular numbered version of this License "or any later version" applies to it, you have the option of following the terms

Poet of the Macabre

and conditions either of that specified version or of any later version that has been published (not as a draft) by the Free Software Foundation. If the Document does not specify a version number of this License, you may choose any version ever published (not as a draft) by the Free Software Foundation.

How to use this License for your documents

To use this License in a document you have written, include a copy of the License in the document and put the following copyright and license notices just after the title page:

Copyright (c) YEAR YOUR NAME.
Permission is granted to copy, distribute and/or modify this document under the terms of the GNU Free Documentation License, Version 1.2 or any later version published by the Free Software Foundation; with no Invariant Sections, no Front-Cover Texts, and no Back-Cover Texts. A copy of the license is included in the section entitled "GNU
Free Documentation License".

If you have Invariant Sections, Front-Cover Texts and Back-Cover Texts, replace the "with...Texts." line with this:

with the Invariant Sections being LIST THEIR TITLES, with the Front-Cover Texts being LIST, and with the Back-Cover Texts being LIST.

If you have Invariant Sections without Cover Texts, or some other combination of the three, merge those two alternatives to suit the situation.

If your document contains nontrivial examples of program code, we recommend releasing these examples in parallel under your choice of free software license, such as the GNU General Public License, to permit their use in free software.

CPSIA information can be obtained at www.ICGtesting.com
Printed in the USA
LVOW030812161011

250669LV00007B/215/P